Freeman-Smith, a division of Worthy Media, Inc.

134 Franklin Road, Suite 200, Brentwood, Tennessee 37027

The quoted ideas expressed in this book (but not Scripture verses) are not, in all cases, exact quotations, as some have been edited for clarity and brevity. In all cases, the author has attempted to maintain the speaker's original intent. In some cases, quoted material for this book was obtained from secondary sources, primarily print media. While every effort was made to ensure the accuracy of these sources, the accuracy cannot be guaranteed. For additions, deletions, corrections, or clarifications in future editions of this text, please write Freeman-Smith.

Scripture quotations are taken from:

The Holy Bible, King James Version (KJV)

The Holy Bible, New International Version (NIV) Copyright © 1973, 1978, 1984, by International Bible Society. Used by permission of Zondervan Publishing House. All rights reserved.

The Holy Bible, New King James Version (NKJV) Copyright © 1982 by Thomas Nelson, Inc. Used by permission.

The New American Standard Bible®, (NASB) Copyright © 1960, 1962, 1963, 1968, 1971, 1972, 1973, 1975, 1977, 1995 by The Lockman Foundation. Used by permission.

The Holman Christian Standard Bible™ (HCSB) Copyright © 1999, 2000, 2001 by Holman Bible Publishers. Used by permission.

Cover Design by Scott Williams/ Richmond & Williams

Page Layout by Bart Dawson

ISBN 978-1-60587-380-0

2 3 4 5 6—RRD—17 16 15 14 13

Printed in China

Sis Kathy-Cathy?

Sis Sally

10 - 25 - 15

I said a prayer for
you today
my friend

Introduction

Because you're reading this book, you undoubtedly have a friend who's praying for you. If so, congratulations. You can be sure that God hears every prayer made on your behalf.

This book is intended to remind you of the love, the prayers, and the principles that concerned friends (like yours) offer to the people they care for. So, during the next 30 days, please try this experiment: read a chapter each day. If you're already committed to a daily worship time, this book will enrich that experience—if not, the simple act of giving God a few minutes each morning will change the direction of your day and the quality of your life.

As you contemplate your own circumstances, remember this: whatever the size of your challenges, God is bigger. Much bigger. He will instruct you, protect you, energize you, and heal you if you let Him. So pray fervently, listen carefully, work diligently, and hope mightily. When you do so, you and your loved ones can expect the best, not only for the day ahead, but also for all eternity.

That our Lord open
the windows of heaven
and pour you out blessings
more than you can hold
and for your husband and
family all be saved
and serving the Lord
with you.

God Bless
Love Ya,

S.S Sally

Amen

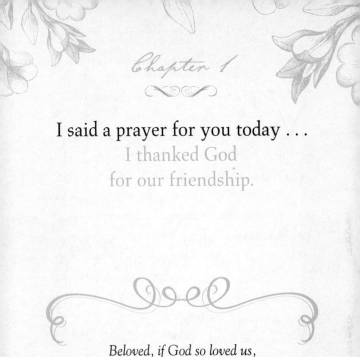

Chapter 1

I said a prayer for you today . . .
I thanked God
for our friendship.

Beloved, if God so loved us,
we also ought to love one another.

—

1 John 4:11 NKJV

THE JOYS OF FRIENDSHIP

What is a friend? The dictionary defines the word *friend* as "a person who is attached to another by feelings of affection or personal regard." This definition is accurate, as far as it goes, but when we examine the deeper meaning of friendship, so many more descriptors come to mind: trustworthiness, loyalty, helpfulness, kindness, understanding, forgiveness, encouragement, humor, and cheerfulness, to mention but a few.

> The best times in life are made a thousand times better when shared with a dear friend.
>
> — Luci Swindoll

Genuine friendships should be treasured, protected, and nourished. And how do we do so? By observing the Golden Rule: As Christians, we are commanded to treat others as we wish to be treated (Matthew 7:12). When we treat others with kindness, courtesy, and respect, we build friendships that last a lifetime. And beyond.

MORE FROM GOD'S WORD

A friend loves at all times, and a brother is born for a difficult time.

Proverbs 17:17 HCSB

Iron sharpens iron, and one man sharpens another.

Proverbs 27:17 HCSB

Finally, all of you be of one mind, having compassion for one another; love as brothers, be tenderhearted, be courteous.

1 Peter 3:8 NKJV

The one who loves his brother remains in the light, and there is no cause for stumbling in him.

1 John 2:10 HCSB

No one has greater love than this, that someone would lay down his life for his friends.

John 15:13 HCSB

MORE GREAT IDEAS

Friendship is the greatest of worldly goods. Certainly to me it is the chief happiness of life. If I had to give a piece of advice to a young man about a place to live, I think I should say, "sacrifice almost everything to live where you can be near your friends." I know I am very fortunate in that respect.

C. S. Lewis

We long to find someone who has been where we've been, who shares our fragile skies, who sees our sunsets with the same shades of blue.

Beth Moore

Inasmuch as anyone pushes you nearer to God, he or she is your friend.

Barbara Johnson

If you choose to awaken a passion for God, you will have to choose your friends wisely.

Lisa Bevere

Friends are like a quilt with lots of different shapes, sizes, colors, and patterns of fabric. But the end result brings you warmth and comfort in a support system that makes your life richer and fuller.

Suzanne Dale Ezell

Perhaps the greatest treasure on earth and one of the only things that will survive this life is human relationships: old friends. We are indeed rich if we have friends. Friends who have loved us through the problems and heartaches of life. Deep, true, joyful friendships. Life is too short and eternity too long to live without old friends.

Gloria Gaither

A TIMELY TIP

Remember that the friends you choose can make a profound impact on every other aspect of your life. So choose carefully and prayerfully.

Chapter 2

I said a prayer for you today . . .

I prayed that your heart
will be touched by God's Word.

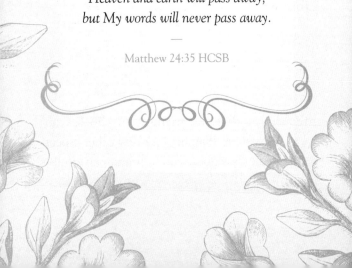

Heaven and earth will pass away,
but My words will never pass away.

—

Matthew 24:35 HCSB

TRUSTING GOD'S PROMISES

God's promises are found in a book like no other: the Holy Bible. The Bible is a road map for life here on earth and for life eternal. As Christians, we are called upon to trust its promises, to follow its commandments, and to share its Good News.

As believers, we must study the Bible daily and meditate upon its meaning for our lives. Otherwise, we deprive ourselves of a priceless gift from our Creator. God's Holy Word is, indeed, a transforming, life-changing, one-of-a-kind treasure. And, a passing acquaintance with the Good Book is insufficient for Christians who seek to obey God's Word and to understand His will.

God has made promises to mankind and to you. God's promises never fail

> Nobody ever outgrows Scripture; the book widens and deepens with our years.
>
> —
>
> C. H. Spurgeon

and they never grow old. You must trust those promises and share them with your family, with your friends, and with the world.

MORE FROM GOD'S WORD

Man shall not live by bread alone, but by every word that proceeds from the mouth of God.

Matthew 4:4 NKJV

For I am not ashamed of the gospel, because it is God's power for salvation to everyone who believes.

Romans 1:16 HCSB

All Scripture is inspired by God and is profitable for teaching, for rebuking, for correcting, for training in righteousness, so that the man of God may be complete, equipped for every good work.

2 Timothy 3:16-17 HCSB

For the word of God is living and effective and sharper than any two-edged sword, penetrating as far as to divide soul, spirit, joints, and marrow; it is a judge of the ideas and thoughts of the heart.

Hebrews 4:12 HCSB

Faith is the virtue that enables us to believe and obey the Word of God, for faith comes from hearing and hearing from the Word of God.

Franklin Graham

God has given us all sorts of counsel and direction in his written Word; thank God, we have it written down in black and white.

John Eldredge

My meditation and study have shown me that, like God, His Word is holy, everlasting, absolutely true, powerful, personally fair, and never changing.

Bill Bright

Words fail to express my love for this holy Book, my gratitude for its author, for His love and goodness. How shall I thank Him for it?

Lottie Moon

Weave the unveiling fabric of God's word through your heart and mind. It will hold strong, even if the rest of life unravels.

Gigi Graham Tchividjian

The Bible became a living book and a guide for my life.

Vonette Bright

God's Word is not merely letters on paper . . . it's alive. Believe and draw near, for it longs to dance in your heart and whisper to you in the night.

Lisa Bevere

A TIMELY TIP

Charles Swindoll writes, "There are four words I wish we would never forget, and they are, 'God keeps his word.'" And remember: When it comes to studying God's Word, school is always in session.

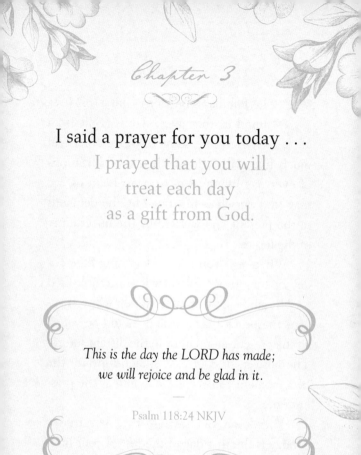

Chapter 3

I said a prayer for you today . . .
I prayed that you will
treat each day
as a gift from God.

*This is the day the LORD has made;
we will rejoice and be glad in it.*

Psalm 118:24 NKJV

TODAY IS THE DAY!

The familiar words of Psalm 118:24 remind us that every day is a gift from God. Yet on some days, we don't feel much like celebrating. When the obligations of everyday living seem to overwhelm us, we may find ourselves frustrated by the demands of the present and worried by the uncertainty of the future.

When will you start celebrating life? Today or tomorrow? When will you thank God for His gifts—now or later? When will you accept the peace that can and should be yours? In the present moment or in the distant future? The answer, of course, is straightforward: the best moment to accept God's gifts is the present one.

There's an old saying—trite but true—"Today is the first day of the rest of your life." Whatever the days ahead may hold, keep God as your partner and Christ as your Savior. And every day, give thanks to the One who created you and saved you. God's love for you is infinite. Accept it joyously and be thankful.

Rejoice in the Lord always. I will say it again: Rejoice!

Philippians 4:4 HCSB

David and the whole house of Israel were celebrating before the Lord.

2 Samuel 6:5 HCSB

Their sorrow was turned into rejoicing and their mourning into a holiday. They were to be days of feasting, rejoicing, and of sending gifts to one another and the poor.

Esther 9:22 HCSB

At the dedication of the wall of Jerusalem, they sent for the Levites wherever they lived and brought them to Jerusalem to celebrate the joyous dedication with thanksgiving and singing accompanied by cymbals, harps, and lyres.

Nehemiah 12:27 HCSB

MORE GREAT IDEAS

If you can forgive the person you were, accept the person you are, and believe in the person you will become, you are headed for joy. So celebrate your life.

Barbara Johnson

Yesterday is the tomb of time, and tomorrow is the womb of time. Only now is yours.

R. G. Lee

Christ is the secret, the source, the substance, the center, and the circumference of all true and lasting gladness.

Mrs. Charles E. Cowman

Jesus intended for us to be overwhelmed by the blessings of regular days. He said it was the reason he had come: "I am come that they might have life, and that they might have it more abundantly."

Gloria Gaither

God gave you this glorious day. Don't disappoint Him. Use it for His glory.

Marie T. Freeman

Submit each day to God, knowing that He is God over all your tomorrows.

Kay Arthur

When the dream of our heart is one that God has planted there, a strange happiness flows into us. At that moment, all of the spiritual resources of the universe are released to help us. Our praying is then at one with the will of God and becomes a channel for the Creator's purposes for us and our world.

Catherine Marshall

A TIMELY TIP

Today is a wonderful, one-of-a-kind gift from God. Treat it that way.

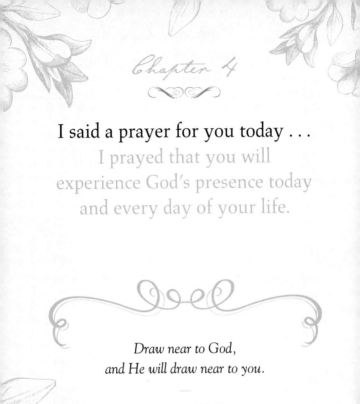

Chapter 4

I said a prayer for you today . . .

I prayed that you will
experience God's presence today
and every day of your life.

*Draw near to God,
and He will draw near to you.*

James 4:8 HCSB

SENSING GOD'S PRESENCE

Since God is everywhere, we are free to sense His presence whenever we take the time to quiet our souls and turn our prayers to Him. But sometimes, amid the incessant demands of everyday life, we turn our thoughts far from God; when we do, we suffer.

Do you set aside quiet moments each day to offer praise to your Creator? As a person who has received the gift of God's grace, you most certainly should. Silence is a gift that you give to yourself and to God. During these moments of stillness, you will often sense the infinite love and power of your Creator—and He, in turn, will speak directly to your heart.

The words of Psalm 46:10 remind us to "be still, and know that I am God." When we do so, we encounter the awesome presence of our loving Father, and we are comforted in the knowledge that God is not just near. He is here.

> If your heart has grown cold, it is because you have moved away from the fire of His presence.
>
> —
>
> Beth Moore

MORE FROM GOD'S WORD

You will seek Me and find Me when you search for Me with all your heart.

Jeremiah 29:13 HCSB

The Lord is near all who call out to Him, all who call out to Him with integrity. He fulfills the desires of those who fear Him; He hears their cry for help and saves them.

Psalm 145:18-19 HCSB

Surely goodness and mercy shall follow me all the days of my life: and I will dwell in the house of the Lord for ever.

Psalm 23:6 KJV

I am not alone, because the Father is with Me.

John 16:32 HCSB

I have set the Lord always before me; because He is at my right hand I shall not be moved.

Psalm 16:8 NKJV

MORE GREAT IDEAS

Give yourself a gift today: be present with yourself. God is. Enjoy your own personality. God does.

Barbara Johnson

Through the death and broken body of Jesus Christ on the Cross, you and I have been given access to the presence of God when we approach Him by faith in prayer.

Anne Graham Lotz

Our souls were made to live in an upper atmosphere, and we stifle and choke if we live on any lower level. Our eyes were made to look off from these heavenly heights, and our vision is distorted by any lower gazing.

Hannah Whitall Smith

It is God to whom and with whom we travel, and while He is the End of our journey, He is also at every stopping place.

Elisabeth Elliot

God wants to be in our leisure time as much as He is in our churches and in our work.

Beth Moore

Oh! what a Savior, gracious to all, / Oh! how His blessings round us fall, / Gently to comfort, kindly to cheer, / Sleeping or waking, God is near.

Fanny Crosby

If you want to hear God's voice clearly and you are uncertain, then remain in His presence until He changes that uncertainty. Often, much can happen during this waiting for the Lord. Sometimes, He changes pride into humility, doubt into faith and peace.

Corrie ten Boom

A TIMELY TIP

If you're here, God is here. If you're there, God is, too. You can't get away from Him or His love . . . thank goodness!

Chapter 5

I said a prayer for you today . . .
I prayed that you will
find strength in God.

And He said to me,
"My grace is sufficient for you,
for My strength is made perfect in weakness."

—

2 Corinthians 12:9 NKJV

STRENGTH FOR THE JOURNEY

Where do you go to find strength? The gym? The health food store? The espresso bar? There's a better source of strength, of course, and that source is God. He is a never-ending source of strength and courage if you call upon Him.

Are you an energized Christian? You should be. But if you're not, you must seek strength and renewal from the source that will never fail: that source, of course, is your Heavenly Father. And rest assured—when you sincerely petition Him, He will give you all the strength you need to live victoriously for Him.

Have you "tapped in" to the power of God? Have you turned your life and your heart over to Him, or are you muddling along under your own power? The answer to this question will determine the quality of your life here on earth and the destiny of your life throughout all eternity. So start tapping in—and remember that when it comes to strength, God is the Ultimate Source.

MORE FROM GOD'S WORD

You, therefore, my child, be strong in the grace that is in Christ Jesus.

2 Timothy 2:1 HCSB

The Lord is my strength and my song; He has become my salvation.

Exodus 15:2 HCSB

He gives strength to the weary and strengthens the powerless.

Isaiah 40:29 HCSB

But those who wait on the Lord shall renew their strength; they shall mount up with wings like eagles, they shall run and not be weary, they shall walk and not faint.

Isaiah 40:31 NKJV

Finally, be strengthened by the Lord and by His vast strength.

Ephesians 6:10 HCSB

MORE GREAT IDEAS

When you and I are related to Jesus Christ, our strength and wisdom and peace and joy and love and hope may run out, but His life rushes in to keep us filled to the brim. We are showered with blessings, not because of anything we have or have not done, but simply because of Him.

Anne Graham Lotz

Hope can give us life. It can provide energy that would otherwise do us in completely if we tried to operate in our own strength.

Barbara Johnson

When the dream of our heart is one that God has planted there, a strange happiness flows into us. At that moment, all of the spiritual resources of the universe are released to help us. Our praying is then at one with the will of God and becomes a channel for the Creator's purposes for us and our world.

Catherine Marshall

Worry does not empty tomorrow of its sorrow; it empties today of its strength.

Corrie ten Boom

Sometimes I think spiritual and physical strength is like manna: you get just what you need for the day, no more.

Suzanne Dale Ezell

One reason so much American Christianity is a mile wide and an inch deep is that Christians are simply tired. Sometimes you need to kick back and rest for Jesus' sake.

Dennis Swanberg

A TIMELY TIP

When you are tired, fearful, or discouraged, God can restore your strength.

Chapter 6

I said a prayer for you today . . .
I prayed that you will
understand the power
of patience.

Rejoice in hope; be patient in affliction;
be persistent in prayer.

—

Romans 12:12 HCSB

THE POWER OF PATIENCE

We human beings are, by our very nature, impatient. We are impatient with others, impatient with ourselves, and impatient with our Creator. We want things to happen according to our own timetables, but our Heavenly Father may have other plans. That's why we must learn the art of patience.

Psalm 37:7 commands us to "rest in the Lord, and wait patiently for Him" (NKJV). But, for most of us, waiting patiently for Him is difficult. Why? Because we are fallible people who seek solutions to our problems today, if not sooner. Still, God instructs us to wait patiently for His plans to unfold, and that's exactly what we should do.

So the next time you find yourself drumming your fingers as you wait for a quick resolution to the challenges of everyday living, take a deep breath and ask God for patience. Be still before your Heavenly Father and trust His timetable: it's the peaceful way to live.

MORE FROM GOD'S WORD

Love is patient; love is kind.

1 Corinthians 13:4 HCSB

A patient spirit is better than a proud spirit.

Ecclesiastes 7:8 HCSB

Therefore the Lord is waiting to show you mercy, and is rising up to show you compassion, for the Lord is a just God. Happy are all who wait patiently for Him.

Isaiah 30:18 HCSB

Be gentle to everyone, able to teach, and patient.

2 Timothy 2:23 HCSB

My brethren, count it all joy when you fall into various trials, knowing that the testing of your faith produces patience. But let patience have its perfect work, that you may be perfect and complete, lacking nothing.

James 1:2-4 NKJV

We must learn to wait. There is grace supplied to the one who waits.

Mrs. Charles E. Cowman

When we read of the great Biblical leaders, we see that it was not uncommon for God to ask them to wait, not just a day or two, but for years, until God was ready for them to act.

Gloria Gaither

Waiting is the hardest kind of work, but God knows best, and we may joyfully leave all in His hands.

Lottie Moon

Let me encourage you to continue to wait with faith. God may not perform a miracle, but He is trustworthy to touch you and make you whole where there used to be a hole.

Lisa Whelchel

Waiting is an essential part of spiritual discipline. It can be the ultimate test of faith.

Anne Graham Lotz

Those who have had to wait and work for happiness seem to enjoy it more, because they never take it for granted.

Barbara Johnson

If you want to hear God's voice clearly and you are uncertain, then remain in His presence until He changes that uncertainty. Often much can happen during this waiting for the Lord. Sometimes he changes pride into humility; doubt into faith and peace.

Corrie ten Boom

A TIMELY TIP

When you learn to be more patient with others, you'll make your world—and your heart—a better place.

Chapter 7

I said a prayer for you today . . .

I prayed that you will focus
your thoughts on
God's infinite blessings,
not on life's inevitable
hardships.

*Finally brothers, whatever is true, whatever is
honorable, whatever is just, whatever is pure,
whatever is lovely, whatever is commendable—if
there is any moral excellence and if there is any
praise—dwell on these things.*

Philippians 4:8 HCSB

OPTIMISM NOW

Pessimism and Christianity don't mix. Why? Because Christians have every reason to be optimistic about life here on earth and life eternal. Mrs. Charles E. Cowman advised, "Never yield to gloomy anticipation. Place your hope and confidence in God. He has no record of failure."

Sometimes, despite our trust in God, we may fall into the spiritual traps of worry, frustration, anxiety, or sheer exhaustion, and our hearts become heavy. What's needed is plenty of rest, a large dose of perspective, and God's healing touch, but not necessarily in that order.

Today, make this promise to yourself and keep it: vow to be a hope-filled Christian. Think optimistically about your life, your profession, and your future. Trust your hopes, not your fears. Take time to celebrate God's glorious creation. And then, when you've filled your heart with hope and gladness, share your optimism with others. They'll be better for it, and so will you. But not necessarily in that order.

MORE FROM GOD'S WORD

Make me hear joy and gladness.

Psalm 51:8 NKJV

My cup runs over. Surely goodness and mercy shall follow me all the days of my life; and I will dwell in the house of the Lord Forever.

Psalm 23:5-6 NKJV

But if we hope for what we do not see, we eagerly wait for it with patience.

Romans 8:25 HCSB

For God has not given us a spirit of fearfulness, but one of power, love, and sound judgment.

2 Timothy 1:7 HCSB

Be strong and courageous, all you who put your hope in the LORD.

Psalm 31:24 HCSB

MORE GREAT IDEAS

The Christian lifestyle is not one of legalistic do's and don'ts, but one that is positive, attractive, and joyful.

Vonette Bright

It never hurts your eyesight to look on the bright side of things.

Barbara Johnson

Christ can put a spring in your step and a thrill in your heart. Optimism and cheerfulness are products of knowing Christ.

Billy Graham

Make the least of all that goes and the most of all that comes. Don't regret what is past. Cherish what you have. Look forward to all that is to come. And most important of all, rely moment by moment on Jesus Christ.

Gigi Graham Tchividjian

We may run, walk, stumble, drive, or fly, but let us never lose sight of the reason for the journey, or miss a chance to see a rainbow on the way.

Gloria Gaither

If you can't tell whether your glass is half-empty or half-full, you don't need another glass; what you need is better eyesight . . . and a more thankful heart.

Marie T. Freeman

Don't miss the beautiful colors of the rainbow while you're looking for the pot of gold at the end of it!

Barbara Johnson

A TIMELY TIP

Be positive: If your thoughts tend toward the negative end of the spectrum, redirect them. How? You can start by counting your blessings and by thanking your Father in heaven.

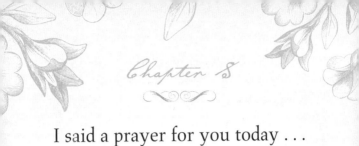

Chapter 8

I said a prayer for you today . . .
I prayed that you will be
quick to forgive everyone,
including yourself.

All bitterness, anger and wrath, insult and
slander must be removed from you, along with all
wickedness. And be kind and compassionate to
one another, forgiving one another, just as God
also forgave you in Christ.

—

Ephesians 4:31-32 HCSB

FORGIVENESS NOW

Forgiveness is seldom easy, but it is always right. When we forgive those who have hurt us, we honor God by obeying His commandments. But when we harbor bitterness against others, we disobey God—with predictably unhappy results.

Are you easily frustrated by the inevitable shortcomings of others? If so, perhaps you need a refresher course in the art of forgiveness.

If there exists even one person, alive or dead, whom you have not forgiven (and that includes yourself), follow God's commandment and His will for your life: forgive that person today. And remember that bitterness, anger, and regret are not part of God's plan for your life. Forgiveness is.

> Give me such love for God and men as will blot out all hatred and bitterness.
>
> —
>
> Dietrich Bonhoeffer

MORE FROM GOD'S WORD

A person's insight gives him patience, and his virtue is to overlook an offense.

Proverbs 19:11 HCSB

See to it that no one repays evil for evil to anyone, but always pursue what is good for one another and for all.

1 Thessalonians 5:15 HCSB

And forgive us our sins, for we ourselves also forgive everyone in debt to us.

Luke 11:4 HCSB

Be merciful, just as your Father also is merciful.

Luke 6:36 HCSB

When they persisted in questioning Him, He stood up and said to them, "The one without sin among you should be the first to throw a stone at her."

John 8:7 HCSB

my friend

MORE GREAT IDEAS

By not forgiving, by not letting wrongs go, we aren't getting back at anyone. We are merely punishing ourselves by barricading our own hearts.

Jim Cymbala

To hold on to hate and resentments is to throw a monkey wrench into the machinery of life.

E. Stanley Jones

God forgets the past. Imitate him.

Max Lucado

Our forgiveness toward others should flow from a realization and appreciation of God's forgiveness toward us.

Franklin Graham

Forgiveness is God's command.

Martin Luther

Forgiveness is the key that unlocks the door of resentment and the handcuffs of hate. It is a power that breaks the chains of bitterness and the shackles of selfishness.

Corrie ten Boom

The love of God is revealed in that He laid down His life for His enemies.

Oswald Chambers

Miracles broke the physical laws of the universe; forgiveness broke the moral rules.

Philip Yancey

A TIMELY TIP

Today, make a list of the people you still need to forgive. Then make up your mind to forgive at least one person on that list. Finally, ask God to cleanse your heart of bitterness, animosity, and regret. If you ask Him sincerely and often, He will respond.

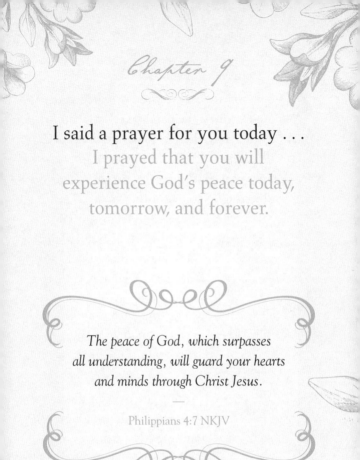

Chapter 9

I said a prayer for you today . . .
I prayed that you will
experience God's peace today,
tomorrow, and forever.

The peace of God, which surpasses
all understanding, will guard your hearts
and minds through Christ Jesus.

—

Philippians 4:7 NKJV

FINDING PEACE

Sometimes, peace can be a scarce commodity in a demanding, 21st-century world. How, then, can we find the peace that we so desperately desire? By slowing down, by keeping problems in perspective, by counting our blessings, and by trusting God.

Dorothy Harrison Pentecost writes, "Peace is full confidence that God is Who He say He is and that He will keep every promise in His Word."

And Beth Moore advises, "Prayer guards hearts and minds and causes God to bring peace out of chaos."

So today, as you journey out into the chaos of the world, bring God's peace with you. And remember: the chaos is temporary, but God's peace is not.

> Peace is
> the deepest thing
> a human
> personality
> can know;
> it is almighty.
>
> —
>
> Oswald Chambers

MORE FROM GOD'S WORD

Abundant peace belongs to those who love Your instruction; nothing makes them stumble.

Psalm 119:165 HCSB

If possible, on your part, live at peace with everyone.

Romans 12:18 HCSB

Blessed are the peacemakers, for they shall be called sons of God.

Matthew 5:9 NKJV

And suddenly there was with the angel a multitude of the heavenly host praising God and saying: "Glory to God in the highest, And on earth peace, goodwill toward men!"

Luke 2:13-14 NKJV

So then, we must pursue what promotes peace and what builds up one another.

Romans 14:19 HCSB

MORE GREAT IDEAS

That peace, which has been described and which believers enjoy, is a participation of the peace which their glorious Lord and Master himself enjoys.

Jonathan Edwards

We're prone to want God to change our circumstances, but He wants to change our character. We think that peace comes from the outside in, but it comes from the inside out.

Warren Wiersbe

Thou hast formed us for Thyself, and our hearts are restless till they find rest in Thee.

St. Augustine

A great many people are trying to make peace, but that has already been done. God has not left it for us to do; all we have to do is to enter into it.

D. L. Moody

What peace can they have who are not at peace with God?

Matthew Henry

He keeps us in perfect peace while He whispers His secrets and reveals His counsels.

Oswald Chambers

Peace with God is where all peace begins.

Jim Gallery

In the center of a hurricane there is absolute quiet and peace. There is no safer place than in the center of the will of God.

Corrie ten Boom

A TIMELY TIP

Do you want to discover God's peace? Then do your best to live in the center of God's will.

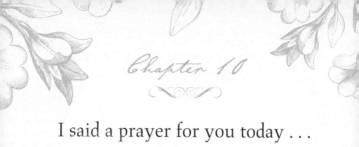

Chapter 10

I said a prayer for you today . . .
I prayed that you will
talk to God early and often.

*Be kindly affectionate to one another with
brotherly love, in honor giving preference to one
another; not lagging in diligence, fervent in spirit,
serving the Lord; rejoicing in hope, patient in
tribulation, continuing steadfastly in prayer.*

—

Romans 12:10-12 NKJV

THE POWER OF PRAYER

The power of prayer": these words are so familiar, yet sometimes we forget what they mean. Prayer is a powerful tool for communicating with our Creator; it is an opportunity to commune with the Giver of all things good. Prayer is not a thing to be taken lightly or to be used infrequently.

All too often, amid the rush of daily life, we may lose sight of God's presence in our lives. Instead of turning to Him for guidance and for comfort, we depend, instead, upon our own resources. To do so is a profound mistake. Prayer should never be reserved for mealtimes or for bedtimes; it should be an ever-present focus in our daily lives.

Today, instead of turning things over in our minds, let us turn them over to God in prayer. Instead of worrying about our decisions, let's trust God to help us make them. Today, let us pray constantly about things great and small. God is listening, and He wants to hear from us. Now.

MORE FROM GOD'S WORD

And everything—whatever you ask in prayer, believing—you will receive.

Matthew 21:22 HCSB

Rejoice always! Pray constantly. Give thanks in everything, for this is God's will for you in Christ Jesus.

1 Thessalonians 5:16-18 HCSB

Therefore I want the men in every place to pray, lifting up holy hands without anger or argument.

1 Timothy 2:8 HCSB

The intense prayer of the righteous is very powerful.

James 5:16 HCSB

Yet He often withdrew to deserted places and prayed.

Luke 5:16 HCSB

Your family and friends need your prayers and you need theirs. And God wants to hear those prayers. So what are you waiting for?

Marie T. Freeman

There is no way that Christians, in a private capacity, can do so much to promote the work of God and advance the kingdom of Christ as by prayer.

Jonathan Edwards

Prayer is never the least we can do; it is always the most!

A. W. Tozer

God knows that we, with our limited vision, don't even know that for which we should pray. When we entrust our requests to him, we trust him to honor our prayers with holy judgment.

Max Lucado

Prayer guards hearts and minds and causes God to bring peace out of chaos.

Beth Moore

Two wings are necessary to lift our souls toward God: prayer and praise. Prayer asks. Praise accepts the answer.

Mrs. Charles E. Cowman

A life growing in its purity and devotion will be a more prayerful life.

E. M. Bounds

Find a place to pray where no one imagines that you are praying. Then, shut the door and talk to God.

Oswald Chambers

A TIMELY TIP

Prayer changes things—and you—so pray.

Chapter 11

I said a prayer for you today . . .
I prayed that you will find courage through God.

The Lord is the One who will go before you.
He will be with you;
He will not leave you or forsake you.
Do not be afraid or discouraged.

—

Deuteronomy 31:8 HCSB

LIVING COURAGEOUSLY

Christians have every reason to live courageously. After all, the ultimate battle has already been fought and won on the cross at Calvary. But, even dedicated followers of Christ may find their courage tested by the inevitable disappointments and tragedies that occur in the lives of believers and non-believers alike.

Every human life is a tapestry of events: some wonderful, some not-so-wonderful, and some downright disheartening. When the storm clouds form overhead and we find ourselves wandering through the dark valley of despair, our faith is stretched, sometimes to the breaking point. But as believers, we can be comforted: Wherever we find ourselves, whether at the top of the mountain or the depths of the valley, God is there, and because He cares for us, we can live courageously.

The next time you find yourself in a fear-provoking situation, remember that God is as near as your next breath, and remember that He offers salvation to His children. He is your shield and your strength; He is your protector and your deliverer. Call upon Him in your hour of need and then be comforted. Whatever your challenge, whatever your trouble, God can handle it. And will.

MORE FROM GOD'S WORD

Be alert, stand firm in the faith, be brave and strong.

1 Corinthians 16:13 HCSB

For God has not given us a spirit of fearfulness, but one of power, love, and sound judgment.

2 Timothy 1:7 HCSB

Haven't I commanded you: be strong and courageous? Do not be afraid or discouraged, for the Lord your God is with you wherever you go.

Joshua 1:9 HCSB

But when Jesus heard it, He answered him, "Don't be afraid. Only believe."

Luke 8:50 HCSB

MORE GREAT IDEAS

There comes a time when we simply have to face the challenges in our lives and stop backing down.

John Eldredge

Down through the centuries, in times of trouble and trial, God has brought courage to the hearts of those who love Him. The Bible is filled with assurances of God's help and comfort in every kind of trouble which might cause fears to arise in the human heart. You can look ahead with promise, hope, and joy.

Billy Graham

Jesus Christ can make the weakest man into a divine dreadnought, fearing nothing.

Oswald Chambers

Take courage. We walk in the wilderness today and in the Promised Land tomorrow.

D. L. Moody

Faith not only can help you through a crisis, it can help you to approach life after the hard times with a whole new perspective. It can help you adopt an outlook of hope and courage through faith to face reality.

John Maxwell

Why rely on yourself and fall? Cast yourself upon His arm. Be not afraid. He will not let you slip. Cast yourself in confidence. He will receive you and heal you.

St. Augustine

Do not let Satan deceive you into being afraid of God's plans for your life.

R. A. Torrey

A TIMELY TIP

If you trust God completely and without reservation, you have every reason on earth—and in heaven—to live courageously. And that's precisely what you should do.

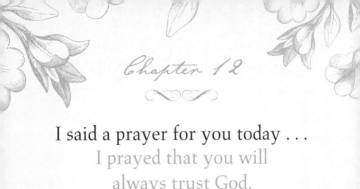

Chapter 12

I said a prayer for you today . . .
I prayed that you will
always trust God.

Trust in the Lord with all your heart,
and do not rely on your own understanding;
think about Him in all your ways,
and He will guide you on the right paths.

—

Proverbs 3:5-6 HCSB

TRUST HIM

When our dreams come true and our plans prove successful, we find it easy to thank our Creator and easy to trust His divine providence. But in times of sorrow or hardship, we may find ourselves questioning God's plans for our lives.

On occasion, you will confront circumstances that trouble you to the very core of your soul. It is during these difficult days that you must find the wisdom and the courage to trust your Heavenly Father despite your circumstances.

Do you seek God's blessings? Then trust Him with your relationships and with your priorities. Follow His commandments and pray for His guidance. Trust your Heavenly Father day by day, moment by moment—in good times and in trying times. Then, wait patiently for God's revelations . . . and prepare yourself for the abundance and peace that will most certainly be yours when you do.

> Never be afraid to trust an unknown future to a known God.
>
> — Corrie ten Boom

MORE FROM GOD'S WORD

For the eyes of the Lord range throughout the earth to show Himself strong for those whose hearts are completely His.

2 Chronicles 16:9 HCSB

He granted their request because they trusted in Him.

1 Chronicles 5:20 HCSB

Let us hold fast the confession of our hope without wavering, for He who promised is faithful.

Hebrews 10:23 NKJV

The one who understands a matter finds success, and the one who trusts in the Lord will be happy.

Proverbs 16:20 HCSB

I know whom I have believed and am persuaded that He is able to guard what has been entrusted to me until that day.

2 Timothy 1:12 HCSB

MORE GREAT IDEAS

Are you serious about wanting God's guidance to become the person he wants you to be? The first step is to tell God that you know you can't manage your own life; that you need his help.

Catherine Marshall

Brother, is your faith looking upward today? / Trust in the promise of the Savior. / Sister, is the light shining bright on your way? / Trust in the promise of thy Lord.

Fanny Crosby

As God's children, we are the recipients of lavish love—a love that motivates us to keep trusting even when we have no idea what God is doing.

Beth Moore

When it is a question of God's almighty Spirit, never say, "I can't."

Oswald Chambers

Do not be afraid, then, that if you trust, or tell others to trust, the matter will end there. Trust is only the beginning and the continual foundation. When we trust Him, the Lord works, and His work is the important part of the whole matter.

Hannah Whitall Smith

When the train goes through a tunnel and the world becomes dark, do you jump out? Of course not. You sit still and trust the engineer to get you through.

Corrie ten Boom

Sometimes the very essence of faith is trusting God in the midst of things He knows good and well we cannot comprehend.

Beth Moore

A TIMELY TIP

One of the most important lessons that you can ever learn is to trust God for everything—not some things, not most things . . . everything!

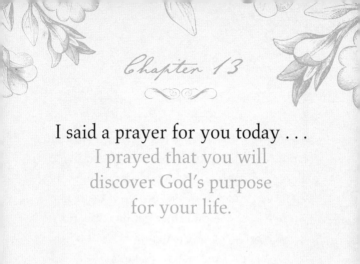

Chapter 13

I said a prayer for you today . . .
I prayed that you will
discover God's purpose
for your life.

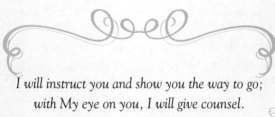

I will instruct you and show you the way to go;
with My eye on you, I will give counsel.

—

Psalm 32:8 HCSB

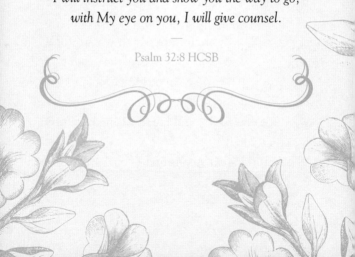

FINDING PURPOSE

Life is best lived on purpose. And purpose, like everything else in the universe, begins with God. Whether you realize it or not, God has a plan for your life, a divine calling, a direction in which He is leading you. When you welcome God into your heart and establish a genuine relationship with Him, He will begin, in time, to make His purposes known.

> Continually restate to yourself what the purpose of your life is.
>
> —
>
> Oswald Chambers

Sometimes, God's intentions will be clear to you; other times, God's plan will seem uncertain at best. But even on those difficult days when you are unsure which way to turn, you must never lose sight of these overriding facts: God created you for a reason; He has important work for you to do; and He's waiting patiently for you to do it.

And the next step is up to you.

MORE FROM GOD'S WORD

We know that all things work together for the good of those who love God: those who are called according to His purpose.

Romans 8:28 HCSB

For it is God who is working among you both the willing and the working for His good purpose.

Philippians 2:13 HCSB

You reveal the path of life to me; in Your presence is abundant joy; in Your right hand are eternal pleasures.

Psalm 16:11 HCSB

In Him we were also made His inheritance, predestined according to the purpose of the One who works out everything in agreement with the decision of His will.

Ephesians 1:11 HCSB

MORE GREAT IDEAS

Without God, life has no purpose, and without purpose, life has no meaning.

Rick Warren

When God speaks to you through the Bible, prayer, circumstances, the church, or in some other way, he has a purpose in mind for your life.

Henry Blackaby and Claude King

Waiting means going about our assigned tasks, confident that God will provide the meaning and the conclusions.

Eugene Peterson

God wants to revolutionize our lives—by showing us how knowing Him can be the most powerful force to help us become all we want to be.

Bill Hybels

The worst thing that laziness does is rob a man of spiritual purpose.

Billy Graham

Whatever purpose motivates your life, it must be something big enough and grand enough to make the investment worthwhile.

Warren Wiersbe

Their distress is due entirely to their deliberate determination to use themselves for a purpose other than God's.

Oswald Chambers

A TIMELY TIP

Ten years from now you will be somewhere—the question is where? You have the power to make that determination. And remember: it's not about earning a living; it's about designing a life.

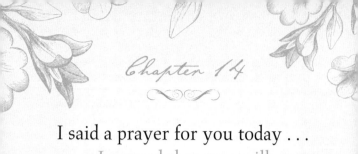

I said a prayer for you today . . .
I prayed that you will
always keep growing both
spiritually and emotionally.

*For this reason also, since the day we heard this,
we haven't stopped praying for you. We are asking
that you may be filled with the knowledge of His
will in all wisdom and spiritual understanding.*

—

Colossians 1:9 HCSB

CONTINUING TO GROW

Whthen will you be a "fully-grown" Christian? Hopefully never—or at least not until you arrive in heaven! As a believer living here on planet earth, you're never "fully grown"; you always have the potential to keep growing.

In those quiet moments when you open your heart to God, the One who made you keeps remaking you. He gives you direction, perspective, wisdom, and courage. And, the appropriate moment to accept those spiritual gifts is always the present one.

Would you like a time-tested formula for spiritual growth? Here it is: keep studying God's Word, keep obeying His commandments, keep praying (and listening for answers), and seek to live in the center of God's will. When you do, you will never be a "stagnant" believer. You will, instead, be a growing Christian . . . and that's precisely the kind of Christian God wants you to be.

MORE FROM GOD'S WORD

But grow in the grace and knowledge of our Lord and Savior Jesus Christ. To Him be the glory both now and to the day of eternity.

2 Peter 3:18 HCSB

I want their hearts to be encouraged and joined together in love, so that they may have all the riches of assured understanding, and have the knowledge of God's mystery—Christ.

Colossians 2:2 HCSB

Therefore, leaving the elementary message about the Messiah, let us go on to maturity.

Hebrews 6:1 HCSB

For You, O God, have tested us; You have refined us as silver is refined. You brought us into the net; You laid affliction on our backs. You have caused men to ride over our heads; we went through fire and through water; but You brought us out to rich fulfillment.

Psalm 66:10-12 NKJV

MORE GREAT IDEAS

We set our eyes on the finish line, forgetting the past, and straining toward the mark of spiritual maturity and fruitfulness.

Vonette Bright

Grow, dear friends, but grow, I beseech you, in God's way, which is the only true way.

Hannah Whitall Smith

We look at our burdens and heavy loads, and we shrink from them. But, if we lift them and bind them about our hearts, they become wings, and on them we can rise and soar toward God.

Mrs. Charles E. Cowman

We should not be upset when unexpected and upsetting things happen. God, in His wisdom, means to make something of us which we have not yet attained, and He is dealing with us accordingly.

J. I. Packer

If all struggles and sufferings were eliminated, the spirit would no more reach maturity than would the child.

Elisabeth Elliot

Having a doctrine pass before the mind is not what the Bible means by knowing the truth. It's only when it reaches down deep into the heart that the truth begins to set us free, just as a key must penetrate a lock to turn it, or as rainfall must saturate the earth down to the roots in order for your garden to grow.

John Eldredge

Salvation is not an event; it is a process.

Henry Blackaby

A TIMELY TIP

When it comes to your faith, God doesn't intend for you to stand still. He wants you to keep moving and growing.

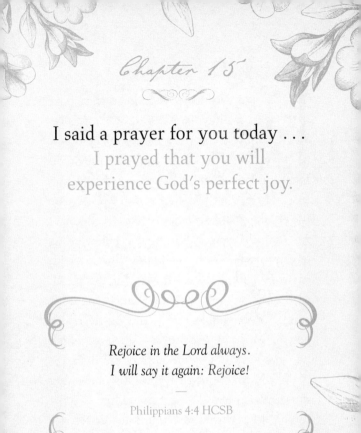

I said a prayer for you today . . .

I prayed that you will
experience God's perfect joy.

Rejoice in the Lord always.
I will say it again: Rejoice!

—

Philippians 4:4 HCSB

REJOICE ALWAYS

Have you made the choice to rejoice? Hopefully so. After all, if you're a believer, you have plenty of reasons to be joyful. Yet sometimes, amid the inevitable hustle and bustle of life here on earth, you may lose sight of your blessings as you wrestle with the challenges of everyday life.

Psalm 100 reminds us that, as believers, we have every reason to celebrate: "Shout for joy to the LORD, all the earth. Worship the LORD with gladness" (vv. 1-2 NIV). Yet sometimes, amid the inevitable hustle and bustle of life here on earth, we can forfeit—albeit temporarily—the joy that God intends for our lives.

If you find yourself feeling discouraged or worse, it's time to slow down and have a quiet conversation with your Creator. If your heart is heavy, open the door of your soul to the Father and to His only begotten Son. Christ offers you His peace and His joy. Accept it and share it freely, just as Christ has freely shared His joy with you.

MORE FROM GOD'S WORD

Now I am coming to You, and I speak these things in the world so that they may have My joy completed in them.

John 17:13 HCSB

Make me to hear joy and gladness.

Psalm 51:8 KJV

So you also have sorrow now. But I will see you again. Your hearts will rejoice, and no one will rob you of your joy.

John 16:22 HCSB

Weeping may spend the night, but there is joy in the morning.

Psalm 30:5 HCSB

Glory in His holy name; let the hearts of those rejoice who seek the Lord! Seek the Lord and His strength; seek His face evermore!

1 Chronicles 16:10-11 NKJV

MORE GREAT IDEAS

Gratitude changes the pangs of memory into a tranquil joy.

Dietrich Bonhoeffer

Joy is the direct result of having God's perspective on our daily lives and the effect of loving our Lord enough to obey His commands and trust His promises.

Bill Bright

Today you will encounter God's creation. When you see the beauty around you, let each detail remind you to lift your head in praise.

Max Lucado

Rejoice, the Lord is King; your Lord and King adore! Rejoice, give thanks and sing and triumph evermore.

Charles Wesley

Joy is the heart's harmonious response to the Lord's song of love.

A. W. Tozer

A life of intimacy with God is characterized by joy.

Oswald Chambers

We all sin by needlessly disobeying the apostolic injunction to rejoice.

C. S. Lewis

The ability to rejoice in any situation is a sign of spiritual maturity.

Billy Graham

A TIMELY TIP

Joy does not depend upon your circumstances, but upon your relationship with God.

Chapter 16

I said a prayer for you today . . .
I prayed that your faith
will be strong.

*For whatever is born of God overcomes the world.
And this is the victory that has overcome
the world—our faith.*

—

1 John 5:4 NKJV

FAITH IN THE FATHER

A suffering woman sought healing in an unusual way: she simply touched the hem of Jesus' garment. When she did, Jesus turned and said, "Daughter, be of good comfort; thy faith hath made thee whole" (Matthew 9:22 KJV). We, too, can be made whole when we place our faith completely and unwaveringly in the person of Jesus Christ.

When you place your faith, your trust, indeed your life in the hands of Christ, you'll be amazed at the marvelous things He can do with you and through you. So strengthen your faith through praise, through worship, through Bible study, and through prayer. Then, trust God's plans. Your Heavenly Father is standing at the door of your heart. If you reach out to Him in faith, He will give you peace and heal your broken spirit. Be content to touch even the smallest fragment of the Master's garment, and He will make you whole.

> If God chooses to remain silent, faith is content.
>
> —
>
> Ruth Bell Graham

MORE FROM GOD'S WORD

Now faith is the reality of what is hoped for, the proof of what is not seen.

Hebrews 11:1 HCSB

Now without faith it is impossible to please God, for the one who draws near to Him must believe that He exists and rewards those who seek Him.

Hebrews 11:6 HCSB

For we walk by faith, not by sight.

2 Corinthians 5:7 HCSB

If you do not stand firm in your faith, then you will not stand at all.

Isaiah 7:9 HCSB

Indeed, God is my salvation. I will trust [Him] and not be afraid. Because Yah, the LORD, is my strength and my song, He has become my salvation.

Isaiah 12:2 HCSB

MORE GREAT IDEAS

Just as our faith strengthens our prayer life, so do our prayers deepen our faith. Let us pray often, starting today, for a deeper, more powerful faith.

Shirley Dobson

Faith does not concern itself with the entire journey. One step is enough.

Mrs. Charles E. Cowman

Grace calls you to get up, throw off your blanket of helplessness, and to move on through life in faith.

Kay Arthur

When you and I place our faith in Jesus Christ and invite Him to come live within us, the Holy Spirit comes upon us, and the power of God overshadows us, and the life of Jesus is born within us.

Anne Graham Lotz

Faith is seeing light with the eyes of your heart, when the eyes of your body see only darkness.

Barbara Johnson

Sometimes the very essence of faith is trusting God in the midst of things He knows good and well we cannot comprehend.

Beth Moore

Faith is nothing more or less than actively trusting God.

Catherine Marshall

A TIMELY TIP

The quality of your faith will help determine the quality of your day and the quality of your life.

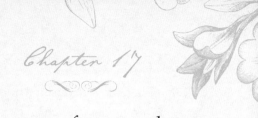

I said a prayer for you today . . .

I prayed that you will
always worship God
with a sincere heart.

*But an hour is coming, and is now here, when
the true worshipers will worship the Father in
spirit and truth. Yes, the Father wants such people
to worship Him. God is Spirit, and those who
worship Him must worship in spirit and truth.*

—

John 4:23-24 HCSB

THE IMPORTANCE OF WORSHIP

Where do we worship? In our hearts or in our church? The answer is both. As Christians who have been saved by a loving, compassionate Creator, we are compelled not only to worship the Creator in our hearts but also to worship Him in the presence of fellow believers.

We live in a world that is teeming with temptations and distractions—a world where good and evil struggle in a constant battle to win our hearts and souls. Our challenge, of course, is to ensure that we cast our lot on the side of God. One way to ensure that we do so is by the practice of regular, purposeful worship with our families. When we worship God faithfully and fervently, we are blessed.

> Worship is not taught from the pulpit. It must be learned in the heart.
>
> —
> Jim Elliot

Worship the Lord your God and . . . serve Him only.

Matthew 4:10 HCSB

So that at the name of Jesus every knee should bow—of those who are in heaven and on earth and under the earth—and every tongue should confess that Jesus Christ is Lord, to the glory of God the Father.

Philippians 2:10-11 HCSB

If anyone is thirsty, he should come to Me and drink!

John 7:37 HCSB

And every day they devoted themselves to meeting together in the temple complex, and broke bread from house to house. They ate their food with gladness and simplicity of heart, praising God and having favor with all the people. And every day the Lord added those being saved to them.

Acts 2:46-47 HCSB

MORE GREAT IDEAS

When God is at the center of your life, you worship. When he's not, you worry.

Rick Warren

Each time, before you intercede, be quiet first and worship God in His glory. Think of what He can do and how He delights to hear the prayers of His redeemed people. Think of your place and privilege in Christ, and expect great things!

Andrew Murray

I am of the opinion that we should not be concerned about working for God until we have learned the meaning and delight of worshipping Him.

A. W. Tozer

Inside the human heart is an undeniable, spiritual instinct to commune with its Creator.

Jim Cymbala

Worship is spiritual. Our worship must be more than just outward expression, it must also take place in our spirits.

Franklin Graham

Worship is a daunting task. Each worships differently. But each should worship.

Max Lucado

Worship is your spirit responding to God's Spirit.

Rick Warren

A TIMELY TIP

Worship reminds you of the awesome power of God. So worship Him daily, and allow Him to work through you every day of the week (not just on Sunday).

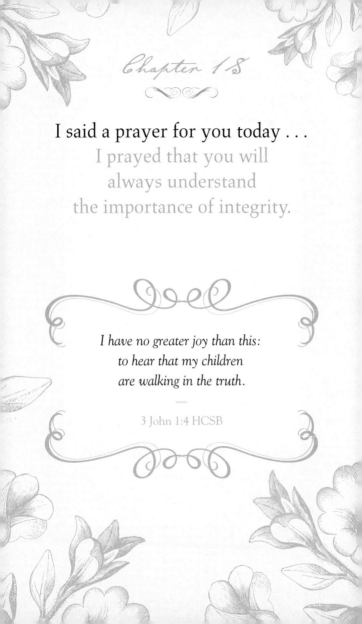

I said a prayer for you today . . .

I prayed that you will
always understand
the importance of integrity.

I have no greater joy than this:
to hear that my children
are walking in the truth.

—

3 John 1:4 HCSB

BUILDING CHARACTER
ONE DAY AT A TIME

Character is built slowly over a lifetime. It is the sum of every right decision, every honest word, every noble thought, and every heartfelt prayer. It is forged on the anvil of honorable work and polished by the twin virtues of generosity and humility. Character is a precious thing—difficult to build but easy to tear down. As believers in Christ, we must seek to live each day with discipline, honesty, and faith. When we do, integrity becomes a habit.

> Character is made in the small moments of our lives.
>
> —
>
> Phillips Brooks

If you sincerely wish to become a righteous person, then you must walk with God and you must follow His commandments. When you do, your character will take care of itself . . . and God will surely smile upon you and yours.

MORE FROM GOD'S WORD

As in water face reflects face, so a man's heart reveals the man.

Proverbs 27:19 NKJV

Do not be deceived: "Evil company corrupts good habits."

1 Corinthians 15:33 NKJV

We also rejoice in our afflictions, because we know that affliction produces endurance, endurance produces proven character, and proven character produces hope.

Romans 5:3-4 HCSB

Now don't be afraid, my daughter. I will do for you whatever you say, since all the people in my town know that you are a woman of noble character.

Ruth 3:11 HCSB

A good name is to be chosen rather than great riches, loving favor rather than silver and gold.

Proverbs 22:1 NKJV

The trials of life can be God's tools for engraving His image on our character.

Warren Wiersbe

There is no way to grow a saint overnight. Character, like the oak tree, does not spring up like a mushroom.

Vance Havner

Character is both developed and revealed by tests, and all of life is a test.

Rick Warren

Integrity is the glue that holds our way of life together. We must constantly strive to keep our integrity intact. When wealth is lost, nothing is lost; when health is lost, something is lost; when character is lost, all is lost.

Billy Graham

Integrity is not a given factor in everyone's life. It is a result of self-discipline, inner trust, and a decision to be relentlessly honest in all situations in our lives.

John Maxwell

Honesty has a beautiful and refreshing simplicity about it. No ulterior motives. No hidden meanings. As honesty and integrity characterize our lives, there will be no need to manipulate others.

Charles Swindoll

The single most important element in any human relationship is honesty—with oneself, with God, and with others.

Catherine Marshall

A TIMELY TIP

Character matters. Your ability to witness for Christ depends more upon your actions than your words.

Chapter 19

I said a prayer for you today . . .

I prayed that you will
always be mindful
of God's blessings.

You will show me the path of life;
in Your presence is fullness of joy;
at Your right hand are pleasures forevermore.

—

Psalm 16:11 NKJV

COUNTING YOUR BLESSINGS

If you sat down and began counting your blessings, how long would it take? A very, very long time! Your blessings include life, freedom, family, friends, talents, and possessions, for starters. But, your greatest blessing—a gift that is yours for the asking—is God's gift of salvation through Christ Jesus.

Are you a thankful believer who takes time each day to take a partial inventory of the gifts God has given you? Hopefully you are that kind of Christian. After all, God's Word makes it clear: a wise heart is a thankful heart.

> God blesses us in spite of our lives and not because of our lives.
>
> —
>
> Max Lucado

Today, begin making a list of your blessings. You most certainly will not be able to make a complete list, but take a few moments and jot down as many blessings as you can. Then, give thanks to the Giver of all good things: God. His love for you is eternal, as are His gifts. And it's never too soon—or too late—to offer Him thanks.

MORE FROM GOD'S WORD

I will make them and the area around My hill a blessing: I will send down showers in their season—showers of blessing.

Ezekiel 34:26 HCSB

Blessed is a man who endures trials, because when he passes the test he will receive the crown of life that He has promised to those who love Him.

James 1:12 HCSB

The Lord bless you and keep you; the Lord make His face shine upon you, and be gracious to you.

Numbers 6:24-25 NKJV

I will make you a great nation; I will bless you and make your name great; and you shall be a blessing. I will bless those who bless you, and I will curse him who curses you; and in you all the families of the earth shall be blessed.

Genesis 12:2-3 NKJV

MORE GREAT IDEAS

God's love for His children is unconditional, no strings attached. But, God's blessings on our lives do come with a condition—obedience. If we are to receive the fullness of God's blessings, we must obey Him and keep His commandments.

Jim Gallery

With the goodness of God to desire our highest welfare and the wisdom of God to plan it, what do we lack? Surely we are the most favored of all creatures.

A. W. Tozer

Get rich quick! Count your blessings!

Anonymous

Blessings can either humble us and draw us closer to God or allow us to become full of pride and self-sufficiency.

Jim Cymbala

Grace is an outrageous blessing bestowed freely on a totally undeserving recipient.

Bill Hybels

The Christian life is motivated, not by a list of do's and don'ts, but by the gracious outpouring of God's love and blessing.

Anne Graham Lotz

It is when we give ourselves to be a blessing that we can specially count on the blessing of God.

Andrew Murray

A TIMELY TIP

God wants to bless you abundantly and eternally. When you trust God completely and obey Him faithfully, you will be blessed.

I said a prayer for you today . . .

I prayed that you will
stay strong
when times are tough.

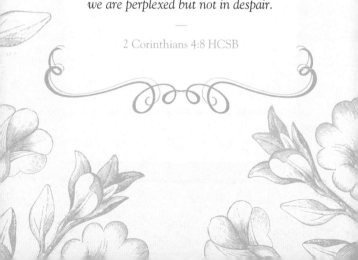

We are pressured in every way but not crushed;
we are perplexed but not in despair.

—

2 Corinthians 4:8 HCSB

ENDURING TOUGH TIMES

From time to time, all of us face adversity, discouragement, or disappointment. And, throughout life, we must all endure life-changing personal losses that leave us breathless. When we do, God stands ready to protect us. Psalm 147 promises, "He heals the brokenhearted, and binds their wounds" (v. 3 NIV).

When we are troubled, we must call upon God, and, in His own time and according to His own plan, He will heal us.

Are you anxious? Take those anxieties to God. Are you troubled? Take your troubles to Him. Does your world seem to be trembling beneath your feet? Seek protection from the One who cannot be moved. The same God who created the universe will protect you if you ask Him . . . so ask Him.

> Measure the size of the obstacles against the size of God.
>
> —
>
> Beth Moore

MORE FROM GOD'S WORD

I called to the Lord in my distress; I called to my God. From His temple He heard my voice.

2 Samuel 22:7 HCSB

Consider it a great joy, my brothers, whenever you experience various trials, knowing that the testing of your faith produces endurance. But endurance must do its complete work, so that you may be mature and complete, lacking nothing.

James 1:2-4 HCSB

When you are in distress and all these things have happened to you, you will return to the Lord your God in later days and obey Him. He will not leave you, destroy you, or forget the covenant with your fathers that He swore to them by oath, because the Lord your God is a compassionate God.

Deuteronomy 4:30-31 HCSB

But as for you, you meant evil against me; but God meant it for good, in order to bring it about as it is this day, to save many people alive.

Genesis 50:20 NKJV

MORE GREAT IDEAS

God will never let you sink under your circumstances. He always provides a safety net and His love always encircles.

Barbara Johnson

If all struggles and sufferings were eliminated, the spirit would no more reach maturity than would the child.

Elisabeth Elliot

Faith is a strong power, mastering any difficulty in the strength of the Lord who made heaven and earth.

Corrie ten Boom

When problems threaten to engulf us, we must do what believers have always done, turn to the Lord for encouragement and solace. As Psalm 46:1 states, "God is our refuge and strength, an ever-present help in trouble."

Shirley Dobson

Even in the winter, even in the midst of the storm, the sun is still there. Somewhere, up above the clouds, it still shines and warms and pulls at the life buried deep inside the brown branches and frozen earth. The sun is there! Spring will come.

Gloria Gaither

God helps those who help themselves, but there are times when we are quite incapable of helping ourselves. That's when God stoops down and gathers us in His arms like a mother lifts a sick child, and does for us what we cannot do for ourselves.

Ruth Bell Graham

A TIMELY TIP

When times are tough, you should guard your heart by turning it over to God.

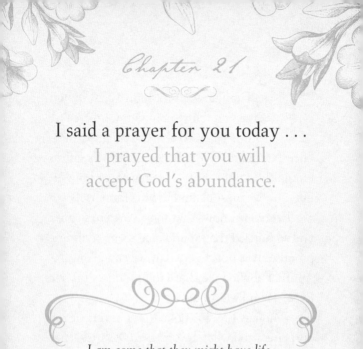

I said a prayer for you today . . .
I prayed that you will
accept God's abundance.

*I am come that they might have life,
and that they might have it more abundantly.*

—

John 10:10 KJV

ACCEPTING GOD'S ABUNDANCE

The familiar words of John 10:10 should serve as a daily reminder: Christ came to this earth so that we might experience His abundance, His love, and His gift of eternal life. But Christ does not force Himself upon us; we must claim His gifts for ourselves.

Everyone knows that some days are so busy and so hurried that abundance seems a distant promise. It is not. Every day, we can claim the spiritual abundance that God promises for our lives . . . and we should.

Thomas Brooks spoke for believers of every generation when he observed, "Christ is the sun, and all the watches of our lives should be set by the dial of his motion." Christ, indeed, is the ultimate Savior of mankind and the personal Savior of those who believe in Him. As His servants, we should place Him at the very center of our lives. And, every day that God gives us breath, we should share Christ's love and His abundance with a world that needs both.

MORE FROM GOD'S WORD

Until now you have asked for nothing in My name. Ask and you will receive, that your joy may be complete.

John 16:24 HCSB

And God is able to make every grace overflow to you, so that in every way, always having everything you need, you may excel in every good work.

2 Corinthians 9:8 HCSB

My cup runs over. Surely goodness and mercy shall follow me all the days of my life; and I will dwell in the house of the Lord forever.

Psalm 23:5-6 NKJV

And He said to them, "Take heed and beware of covetousness, for one's life does not consist in the abundance of the things he possesses."

Luke 12:15 NKJV

MORE GREAT IDEAS

Yes, we were created for His holy pleasure, but we will ultimately—if not immediately—find much pleasure in His pleasure.

Beth Moore

It would be wrong to have a "poverty complex," for to think ourselves paupers is to deny either the King's riches or to deny our being His children.

Catherine Marshall

God's riches are beyond anything we could ask or even dare to imagine! If my life gets gooey and stale, I have no excuse.

Barbara Johnson

The gift of God is eternal life, spiritual life, abundant life through faith in Jesus Christ, the Living Word of God.

Anne Graham Lotz

Jesus intended for us to be overwhelmed by the blessings of regular days. He said it was the reason he had come: "I am come that they might have life, and that they might have it more abundantly."

Gloria Gaither

Get ready for God to show you not only His pleasure, but His approval.

Joni Eareckson Tada

God is the giver, and we are the receivers. And His richest gifts are bestowed not upon those who do the greatest things, but upon those who accept His abundance and His grace.

Hannah Whitall Smith

A TIMELY TIP

Don't miss out on God's abundance. Every day is a beautifully wrapped gift from God. Unwrap it; use it; and give thanks to the Giver.

I said a prayer for you today . . .

I prayed that you will
never lose your
enthusiasm for life.

*Whatever you do, do it enthusiastically,
as something done for the Lord
and not for men.*

—

Colossians 3:23 HCSB

ENTHUSIASM FOR THE JOURNEY

Genuine, heartfelt, enthusiastic Christianity is contagious. If you enjoy a life-altering relationship with God, that relationship will have an impact on others—perhaps a profound impact.

Do you see each day as a glorious opportunity to serve God and to do His will? Are you enthused about life, or do you struggle through each day giving scarcely a thought to God's blessings? Are you constantly praising God for His gifts, and are you sharing His Good News with the world? And are you excited about the possibilities for service that God has placed before you, whether at home, at work, at church, or at school? You should be.

> Enthusiasm, like the flu, is contagious—we get it from one another.
>
> —
>
> Barbara Johnson

You are the recipient of Christ's sacrificial love. Accept it enthusiastically and share it fervently. Jesus deserves your enthusiasm; the world deserves it; and you deserve the experience of sharing it.

MORE FROM GOD'S WORD

I have seen that there is nothing better than for a person to enjoy his activities, because that is his reward. For who can enable him to see what will happen after he dies?

Ecclesiastes 3:22 HCSB

Do not lack diligence; be fervent in spirit; serve the Lord.

Romans 12:11 HCSB

He did it with all his heart. So he prospered.

2 Chronicles 31:21 NKJV

This is the day the Lord has made; let us rejoice and be glad in it.

Psalm 118:24 HCSB

Render service with a good attitude, as to the Lord and not to men.

Ephesians 6:7 HCSB

MORE GREAT IDEAS

Your light is the truth of the Gospel message itself as well as your witness as to Who Jesus is and what He has done for you. Don't hide it.

Anne Graham Lotz

Making up a string of excuses is usually harder than doing the work.

Marie T. Freeman

Wouldn't it make an astounding difference, not only in the quality of the work we do, but also in the satisfaction, even our joy, if we recognized God's gracious gift in every single task?

Elisabeth Elliot

We urgently need people who encourage and inspire us to move toward God and away from the world's enticing pleasures.

Jim Cymbala

Living life with a consistent spiritual walk deeply influences those we love most.

Vonette Bright

Jesus wants Life for us, Life with a capital L.

Criswell Freeman

I don't know about you, but I want to do more than survive life—I want to mount up like the eagle and glide over rocky crags, nest in the tallest of trees, dive for nourishment in the deepest of mountain lakes, and soar on the wings of the wind.

Barbara Johnson

A TIMELY TIP

Don't wait for enthusiasm to find you . . . go looking for it. Look at your life and your relationships as exciting adventures. Don't wait for life to spice up itself; spice things up yourself.

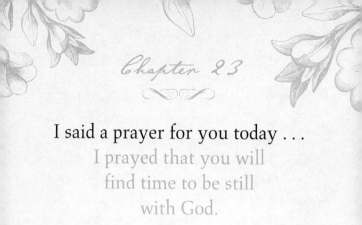

Chapter 23

I said a prayer for you today . . .
I prayed that you will
find time to be still
with God.

Be still, and know that I am God.

Psalm 46:10 KJV

BE STILL

We live in a noisy world, a world filled with distractions, frustrations, and complications. But if we allow the distractions of a clamorous world to separate us from God's peace, we do ourselves a profound disservice. If we are to maintain righteous minds and compassionate hearts, we must take time each day for prayer and for meditation. We must make ourselves still in the presence of our Creator. We must quiet our minds and our hearts so that we might sense God's will, God's love, and God's Son.

> Be quiet enough to hear God's whisper.
>
> —
>
> Anonymous

Has the busy pace of life robbed you of the peace that might otherwise be yours through Jesus Christ? Nothing is more important than the time you spend with your Savior. So be still and claim the inner peace that is your spiritual birthright: the peace of Jesus Christ. It is offered freely; it has been paid for in full; it is yours for the asking. So ask. And then share.

my friend

MORE FROM GOD'S WORD

Be silent before Me.

Isaiah 41:1 HCSB

Be silent before the Lord and wait expectantly for Him.

Psalm 37:7 HCSB

Truly my soul silently waits for God; from Him comes my salvation.

Psalm 62:1 NKJV

My soul, wait silently for God alone, For my expectation is from Him.

Psalm 62:5 NKJV

But those who wait on the Lord shall renew their strength; they shall mount up with wings like eagles, they shall run and not be weary, they shall walk and not faint.

Isaiah 40:31 NKJV

MORE GREAT IDEAS

When we are in the presence of God, removed from distractions, we are able to hear him more clearly, and a secure environment has been established for the young and broken places in our hearts to surface.

John Eldredge

The world is full of noise. Might we not set ourselves to learn silence, stillness, solitude?

Elisabeth Elliot

Because Jesus Christ is our Great High Priest, not only can we approach God without a human "go-between," we can also hear and learn from God in some sacred moments without one.

Beth Moore

I need the spiritual revival that comes from spending quiet time alone with Jesus in prayer and in thoughtful meditation on His Word.

Anne Graham Lotz

Quiet time is giving God your undivided attention for a predetermined amount of time for the purpose of talking to and hearing from Him.

Charles Stanley

In the center of a hurricane there is absolute quiet and peace. There is no safer place than in the center of the will of God.

Corrie ten Boom

Instead of waiting for the feeling, wait upon God. You can do this by growing still and quiet, then expressing in prayer what your mind knows is true about Him, even if your heart doesn't feel it at this moment.

Shirley Dobson

A TIMELY TIP

Be still and listen to God. He has something important to say to you.

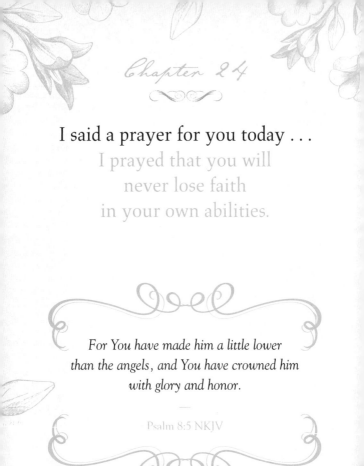

I said a prayer for you today . . .

I prayed that you will
never lose faith
in your own abilities.

*For You have made him a little lower
than the angels, and You have crowned him
with glory and honor.*

Psalm 8:5 NKJV

BELIEVE IN YOURSELF!

o you believe that you deserve the best and that you can achieve the best? Or have you convinced yourself that you're a second-tier talent who'll be lucky to finish far back in the pack? Before you answer that question, remember this: God sent His Son so that you might enjoy the abundant life that Jesus describes in the familiar words of John 10:10. But, God's gifts are not guaranteed—it's up to you to claim them.

As you plan for the next stage of your life's journey, promise yourself that when it comes to the important things in life, you won't settle for second best. And what, pray tell, are the "important things"? Your faith, your family, your health, and your relationships, for starters. In each of these areas, you deserve to be a rip-roaring, top-drawer success.

So if you want to achieve the best that life has to offer, convince yourself that you have the ability to earn all the rewards that God has in store for you. Become sold on yourself—sold on your opportunities, sold on your potential, sold on your abilities. If you're sold on yourself, chances are the world will soon become sold too, and the results will be beautiful.

MORE FROM GOD'S WORD

How happy are those whose way is blameless, who live according to the law of the Lord! Happy are those who keep His decrees and seek Him with all their heart.

Psalm 119:1-2 HCSB

Happy is the one whose help is the God of Jacob, whose hope is in the Lord his God.

Psalm 146:5 HCSB

For it was You who created my inward parts; You knit me together in my mother's womb. I will praise You, because I have been remarkably and wonderfully made. Your works are wonderful, and I know [this] very well.

Psalm 139:13-14 HCSB

MORE GREAT IDEAS

When it comes to our position before God, we're perfect. When he sees each of us, he sees one who has been made perfect through the One who is perfect—Jesus Christ.

Max Lucado

Being loved by Him whose opinion matters most gives us the security to risk loving, too— even loving ourselves.

Gloria Gaither

Give yourself a gift today: be present with yourself. God is. Enjoy your own personality. God does.

Barbara Johnson

The Creator has made us each one of a kind. There is nobody else exactly like us, and there never will be. Each of us is his special creation and is alive for a distinctive purpose.

Luci Swindoll

Comparison is the root of all feelings of inferiority.

James Dobson

If you can forgive the person you were, accept the person you are, and believe in the person you will become, you are headed for joy. So celebrate your life.

Barbara Johnson

I was learning something important: we are most vulnerable to the piercing winds of doubt when we distance ourselves from the mission and fellowship to which Christ has called us. Our night of discouragement will seem endless and our task impossible, unless we recognize that He stands in our midst.

Joni Eareckson Tada

A TIMELY TIP

Old-fashioned respect never goes out of style—respect for other people and respect for the person in the mirror.

I said a prayer for you today . . .

I prayed that you will receive
God's perfect love.

But God demonstrates His own love toward us,
in that while we were still sinners,
Christ died for us.

—

Romans 5:8 NKJV

GOD'S LOVE

You know the profound love that you hold in your heart for your family and friends. As a child of God, you can only imagine the infinite love that your Heavenly Father has for you.

Today, what will you do in response to God's love? Will you live purposefully and joyfully? Will you celebrate God's creation while giving thanks for His blessings? And will you share God's love with family members, friends, and even strangers? Hopefully so. After all, God's message—and His love—are meant to be shared.

Your Heavenly Father—a God of infinite love and mercy—is waiting to embrace you with open arms. Accept His love, and share it, today . . . and forever.

> God loves us the way we are, but He loves us too much to leave us that way.
>
> —
>
> Leighton Ford

MORE FROM GOD'S WORD

May he be blessed by the Lord, who has not forsaken his kindness to the living or the dead.

Ruth 2:20 HCSB

For God loved the world in this way: He gave His only Son, so that everyone who believes in Him will not perish but have eternal life.

John 3:16 HCSB

Whoever is wise will observe these things, and they will understand the lovingkindness of the Lord.

Psalm 107:43 NKJV

But God, who is abundant in mercy, because of His great love that He had for us, made us alive with the Messiah even though we were dead in trespasses. By grace you are saved!

Ephesians 2:4-5 HCSB

We love Him because He first loved us.

1 John 4:19 NKJV

MORE GREAT IDEAS

There is no pit so deep that God's love is not deeper still.

Corrie ten Boom

I love Him because He first loved me, and He still does love me, and He will love me forever and ever.

Bill Bright

The hope we have in Jesus is the anchor for the soul—something sure and steadfast, preventing drifting or giving way, lowered to the depth of God's love.

Franklin Graham

I think God knew that the message we sometimes need to hear today is not what a great and mighty God we serve, but rather what a tender, loving Father we have, even when He says no.

Lisa Whelchel

It broke the heart of God to demonstrate His love to us through Christ, but its ultimate end was salvation.

Beth Moore

Every tiny bit of my life that has value I owe to the redemption of Jesus Christ. Am I doing anything to enable Him to bring His redemption into evident reality in the lives of others?

Oswald Chambers

It was not the soldiers who killed him, nor the screams of the mob: It was his devotion to us.

Max Lucado

A TIMELY TIP

Demonstrate the importance of your relationship with God by spending time with Him each day. And take time each day to share God's love with your family and friends.

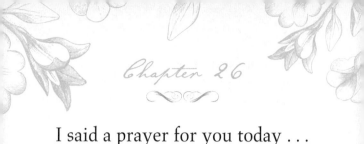

Chapter 26

I said a prayer for you today . . .

I prayed that you will
always stay strong
and never lose hope.

*For I know the thoughts that I think toward you,
says the Lord, thoughts of peace and not of evil,
to give you a future and a hope.
Then you will call upon Me and go
and pray to Me, and I will listen to you.*

Jeremiah 29:11-12 NKJV

BE HOPEFUL

Have you ever felt hope for the future slipping away? If so, you have temporarily lost sight of the hope that we, as believers, must place in the promises of our Heavenly Father. If you are feeling discouraged, worried, or worse, remember the words of Psalm 31: "Be of good courage, and He shall strengthen your heart" (v. 24 NKJV).

Because we are saved by a risen Christ, we can have hope for the future, no matter how desperate our circumstances may seem. After all, God has promised that we are His throughout eternity. And, He has told us that we must place our hopes in Him.

> Our hope in Christ for the future is the mainstream of our joy.
>
> —
>
> C. H. Spurgeon

Of course, we will face disappointments and failures, but these are only temporary defeats. Of course, this world can be a place of trials and tribulations, but we are secure. God has promised us peace, joy, and eternal life. And God keeps His promises today, tomorrow, and forever.

MORE FROM GOD'S WORD

Now may the God of hope fill you with all joy and peace in believing, so that you may overflow with hope by the power of the Holy Spirit.

Romans 15:13 HCSB

But if we hope for what we do not see, we eagerly wait for it with patience.

Romans 8:25 HCSB

Rejoice in hope; be patient in affliction; be persistent in prayer.

Romans 12:12 HCSB

Lord, I turn my hope to You. My God, I trust in You. Do not let me be disgraced; do not let my enemies gloat over me.

Psalm 25:1-2 HCSB

Let us hold on to the confession of our hope without wavering, for He who promised is faithful.

Hebrews 10:23 HCSB

MORE GREAT IDEAS

People are genuinely motivated by hope, and a part of that hope is the assurance of future glory with God for those who are His people.

Warren Wiersbe

I wish I could make it all new again; I can't. But God can. "He restores my soul," wrote the shepherd. God doesn't reform; he restores. He doesn't camouflage the old; he restores the new. The Master Builder will pull out the original plan and restore it. He will restore the vigor, he will restore the energy. He will restore the hope. He will restore the soul.

Max Lucado

Oh, remember this: There is never a time when we may not hope in God. Whatever our necessities, however great our difficulties, and though to all appearance help is impossible, yet our business is to hope in God, and it will be found that it is not in vain.

George Mueller

Through all of the crises of life—and we all are going to experience them—we have this magnificent Anchor.

Franklin Graham

Faith looks back and draws courage; hope looks ahead and keeps desire alive.

John Eldredge

Hope is nothing more than the expectation of those things which faith has believed to be truly promised by God.

John Calvin

A TIMELY TIP

If you're experiencing hard times, you'll be wise to start spending more time with God. And if you do your part, God will do His part. So never be afraid to hope—or to ask—for a miracle.

I said a prayer for you today . . .

I prayed that you will always
find time to praise God.

Praise the Lord, all nations! Glorify Him,
all peoples! For great is His faithful love to us;
the Lord's faithfulness endures forever.
Hallelujah!

—

Psalm 117 HCSB

PRAISE HIM EVERY DAY

When is the best time to praise God? In church? Before dinner is served? When we tuck little children into bed? None of the above. The best time to praise God is all day, every day, to the greatest extent we can, with thanksgiving in our hearts.

Too many of us, even well-intentioned believers, tend to "compartmentalize" our waking hours into a few familiar categories: work, rest, play, family time, and worship. To do so is a mistake. Worship and praise should be woven into the fabric of everything we do; it should never be relegated to a weekly three-hour visit to church on Sunday morning.

Mrs. Charles E. Cowman, the author of the classic devotional text, *Streams in the Desert*, wrote, "Two wings are necessary to lift our souls toward God: prayer and praise. Prayer asks. Praise accepts the answer." Today, find a little more time to lift your concerns to God in prayer, and praise Him for all that He has done. He's listening . . . and He wants to hear from you.

Therefore, through Him let us continually offer up to God a sacrifice of praise, that is, the fruit of our lips that confess His name.

Hebrews 13:15 HCSB

But I will hope continually and will praise You more and more.

Psalm 71:14 HCSB

So that at the name of Jesus every knee should bow—of those who are in heaven and on earth and under the earth—and every tongue should confess that Jesus Christ is Lord, to the glory of God the Father.

Philippians 2:10-11 HCSB

Enter into his gates with thanksgiving, and into his courts with praise: be thankful unto him, and bless his name. For the LORD is good; his mercy is everlasting; and his truth endureth to all generations.

Psalm 100:4-5 KJV

MORE GREAT IDEAS

Why wait until the fourth Thursday in November? Why wait until the morning of December twenty-fifth? Thanksgiving to God should be an everyday affair. The time to be thankful is now!

Jim Gallery

The words "thank" and "think" come from the same root word. If we would think more, we would thank more.

Warren Wiersbe

Thank God every morning when you get up that you have something to do that day which must be done, whether you like it or not.

Charles Kingsley

A child of God should be a visible beatitude for joy and a living doxology for gratitude.

C. H. Spurgeon

It is only with gratitude that life becomes rich.

Dietrich Bonhoeffer

Praise reestablishes the proper chain of command; we recognize that the King is on the throne and that he has saved his people.

Max Lucado

Praise is the highest occupation of any being.

Max Lucado

Holy, holy, holy! Lord God Almighty! All Thy works shall praise Thy name in earth, and sky, and sea.

Reginald Heber

A TIMELY TIP

When you pray, don't just ask God for things—also take time to praise Him.

Chapter 28

I said a prayer for you today . . .
I prayed that you will
turn all your worries
over to God.

*Don't worry about anything, but in everything,
through prayer and petition with thanksgiving,
let your requests be made known to God.*

—

Philippians 4:6 HCSB

Here's a riddle: What is it that is too unimportant to pray about yet too big for God to handle? The answer, of course, is: "nothing." Yet sometimes, when the challenges of the day seem overwhelming, we may spend more time worrying about our troubles than praying about them. And, we may spend more time fretting about our problems than solving them. A far better strategy is to pray as if everything depended entirely upon God and to work as if everything depended entirely upon us.

What we see as problems God sees as opportunities. And if we are to trust Him completely, we must acknowledge that even when our own vision is dreadfully impaired, His vision is perfect.

Today and every day, let us trust God by courageously confronting the things that we see as problems and He sees as possibilities. And while we're at it, let's remind our friends and family members that no problem is too big for God . . . not even our problems.

MORE FROM GOD'S WORD

*Your heart must not be troubled. Believe in God;
believe also in Me.*

John 14:1 HCSB

*Come to Me, all you who labor and are heavy
laden, and I will give you rest. Take My yoke upon
you and learn from Me, for I am gentle and lowly
in heart, and you will find rest for your souls. For
My yoke is easy and My burden is light.*

Matthew 11:28-30 NKJV

*I will be with you when you pass through the waters
. . . when you walk through the fire . . . the flame
will not burn you. For I the Lord your God, the
Holy One of Israel, and your Savior.*

Isaiah 43:2-3 HCSB

*Don't worry about your life, what you will eat or
what you will drink; or about your body, what you
will wear. Isn't life more than food and the body
more than clothing?*

Matthew 6:25 HCSB

MORE GREAT IDEAS

God is bigger than your problems. Whatever worries press upon you today, put them in God's hands and leave them there.

Billy Graham

The beginning of anxiety is the end of faith, and the beginning of true faith is the end of anxiety.

George Mueller

Worry is the senseless process of cluttering up tomorrow's opportunities with leftover problems from today.

Barbara Johnson

Today is mine. Tomorrow is none of my business. If I peer anxiously into the fog of the future, I will strain my spiritual eyes so that I will not see clearly what is required of me now.

Elisabeth Elliott

We are not called to be burden-bearers, but cross-bearers and light-bearers. We must cast our burdens on the Lord.

Corrie ten Boom

We know so little about the future that to worry about it would be the height of foolishness.

C. H. Spurgeon

Worry and anxiety are sand in the machinery of life; faith is the oil.

E. Stanley Jones

Today is the tomorrow we worried about yesterday.

Dennis Swanberg

A TIMELY TIP

An important part of becoming a more mature Christian is learning to worry less and to trust God more.

I said a prayer for you today . . .

I prayed that you will
always know how much
you are loved.

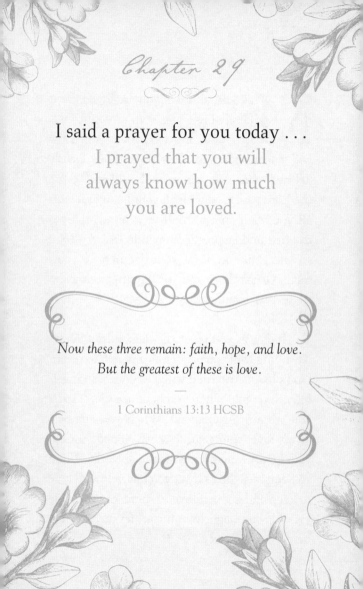

Now these three remain: faith, hope, and love.
But the greatest of these is love.

—

1 Corinthians 13:13 HCSB

YOU ARE LOVED

Make no mistake: you are loved. Your family loves you, your closest friends love you, and God loves you. How will you respond to their love? Jesus clearly defined what your response should be: "'Love the Lord your God with all your heart and with all your soul and with all your mind.' This is the first and greatest commandment. And the second is like it: 'Love your neighbor as yourself.' All the Law and the Prophets hang on these two commandments" (Matthew 22:37-40 NIV).

Today, as you meet the demands of everyday living, will you pause long enough to return God's love? And then will you share it? Prayerfully, you will. When you embrace God's love, you are forever changed. When you embrace God's love, you feel differently about yourself, your family, your friends, and your world. When you embrace God's love, you have enough love to keep and enough love to share: enough love for a day, enough love for a lifetime, enough love for all eternity.

MORE FROM GOD'S WORD

I pray that you, being rooted and firmly established in love, may be able to comprehend with all the saints what is the breadth and width, height and depth, and to know the Messiah's love that surpasses knowledge, so you may be filled with all the fullness of God.

Ephesians 3:17-19 HCSB

If I speak the languages of men and of angels, but do not have love, I am a sounding gong or a clanging cymbal.

1 Corinthians 13:1 HCSB

Dear friends, if God loved us in this way, we also must love one another.

1 John 4:11 HCSB

Above all, keep your love for one another at full strength, since love covers a multitude of sins.

1 Peter 4:8 HCSB

MORE GREAT IDEAS

Love is not soft as water is; it is solid as a rock on which the waves of hatred beat in vain.

Corrie ten Boom

Love always means sacrifice.

Elisabeth Elliot

Line by line, moment by moment, special times are etched into our memories in the permanent ink of everlasting love in our relationships.

Gloria Gaither

Prayer is the ultimate love language. It communicates in ways we can't.

Stormie Omartian

Agape is a kind of love God demonstrates to one person through another.

Beth Moore

Love is extravagant in the price it is willing to pay, the time it is willing to give, the hardships it is willing to endure, and the strength it is willing to spend. Love never thinks in terms of "how little," but always in terms of "how much." Love gives, love knows, and love lasts.

Joni Eareckson Tada

Love is the seed of all hope. It is the enticement to trust, to risk, to try, and to go on.

Gloria Gaither

Forgiveness is the precondition of love.

Catherine Marshall

A TIMELY TIP

God is love, and He expects us to share His love.

Chapter 30

I said a prayer for you today . . .

I prayed that you will receive
God's perfect love.

For the Lord is good, and His love is eternal;
His faithfulness endures through all generations.

—

Psalm 100:5 HCSB

EMBRACED BY GOD

God's love for you is bigger and better than you can imagine. In fact, God's love is far too big to comprehend (in this lifetime). But this much we know: God loves you so much that He sent His Son Jesus to come to this earth and to die for you. And, when you accepted Jesus into your heart, God gave you a gift that is more precious than gold: the gift of eternal life.

The words of Romans 8 make this promise: "For I am persuaded that neither death nor life, nor angels nor principalities nor powers, nor things present nor things to come, nor height nor depth, nor any other created thing, shall be able to separate us from the love of God which is in Christ Jesus our Lord" (vv. 38-39 NKJV).

Sometimes, in the crush of your daily duties, God may seem far away, but He is not. God is everywhere you have ever been and everywhere you will ever go. He is with you night and day; He knows your thoughts and He hears your prayers. When you earnestly seek Him, you will find Him because He is here, waiting patiently for you to reach out to Him.

MORE FROM GOD'S WORD

For God so loved the world, that he gave his only begotten Son, that whosoever believeth in him should not perish, but have everlasting life.

John 3:16 KJV

[Because of] the Lord's faithful love we do not perish, for His mercies never end. They are new every morning; great is Your faithfulness!

Lamentations 3:22-23 HCSB

Help me, Lord my God; save me according to Your faithful love.

Psalm 109:26 HCSB

Whoever is wise will observe these things, and they will understand the lovingkindness of the Lord.

Psalm 107:43 NKJV

A person's insight gives him patience, and his virtue is to overlook an offense.

Proverbs 19:11 HCSB

When I consider my existence beyond the grace, I am filled with confidence and gratitude because God has made an inviolable commitment to take me to heaven on the merits of Christ.

Bill Hybels

When you experience grace and are loved when you do not deserve it, you spend the rest of your life standing on tiptoes trying to reach His plan for your life out of gratitude

Charles Stanley

Jesus loves us with fidelity, purity, constancy, and passion, no matter how imperfect we are.

Stormie Omartian

If we only believe and ask, a full measure of God's grace is available to any of us.

Charles Swindoll

God shares himself generously and graciously.

Eugene Peterson

No one is beyond his grace. No situation, anywhere on earth, is too hard for God.

Jim Cymbala

God's grand strategy, birthed in his grace toward us in Christ, and nurtured through the obedience of disciplined faith, is to release us into the redeemed life of our heart, knowing it will lead us back to him even as the North Star guides a ship across the vast unknown surface of the ocean.

John Eldredge

A TIMELY TIP

God offers you life abundant and life eternal. Accept His gift today.